Serviccceeee Pleassse!!!!!
(That got your attention lol)

Hello everyone and welcome to my very first cookbook

I have spent a number of years finding inspiration in all things food. Whether it's from my younger days watching my mum cook for friends and family (she seems to think that because she gave birth to me, these are her recipes, so technically this is her book... absolute genius), to being glued to Ready Steady Cook on the TV after school (Ainsley Harriot is my hero), to posting my own creations on social media and learning the tricks of the trade right through to working in commercial kitchens, it's safe to say that I have been a foodie for all of my life.

So.. to save you the hassle of working in a busy kitchen for 14 hours a day, I present to you some of my creations that you can put your own twist on at home and become a chef overnight.

Whether you're a budding novice, a seasoned chef looking for something new to season, or you've bagged yourself a date and a chippy tea just won't cut it, there's something here for everyone.

Thank you so much for supporting my book, and I hope you have as much fun in the kitchen with these recipes as I did creating them.

God Bless and Lots of Love x

Ricky

In Memory of Chef Propser Nkomo ...
I still refuse to put soy sauce in an Indian curry bro haha

SPICY TAGLIATELLE BOLOGNESE

 2-4 servings   1 hour and 30 minutes

Ingredients:

For the Pasta:
2 Eggs
200g 00 Flour

For the Bolognese:
500g Quality Minced Beef
2 tbsp Olive Oil
Half a White
Half a Red Onion
4 Cloves of Garlic
Fresh Rosemary
Chopped Fresh Parsley
1 Stick Celery
1 Large Carrot
Good Quality Beer
Coarse Grain Mustard
Good Quality Beef Stock
1 Scotch Bonnet Pepper
1 tsp Cayenne Pepper
100ml of Milk
500ml Passata
5 Small Vine Ripened Tomatoes
2 tsp Dark Soy Sauce
Salt and Pepper to taste and plenty of grated parmesan.

Steps for Cooking:

Pasta

1.Pour 180g of the flour onto a wooden board (keep 20g aside in case your dough is too moist at the end) and make a well in the centre crack the eggs into the well and slowly incorporate a bit of the flour at a time using a fork until everything is incorporated, then use a spatula to form into a dough. Then, using your hands, work the dough until it is smooth and elastic, then cover in cling film and put in the fridge for 30 minutes.

2.Next, unwrap the dough and flatten it out on a well-floured wooden board with a rolling pin. Roll into pasta sheets at 1mm thick, then fold the sheets back on themselves and cut into 3 quarter cm strips. Roll the cut tagliatelle into little nests and sprinkle generously with flour so they don't stick.

Bolognese

1.Chop your onions, garlic, carrots and celery into fine dice. Get your oil in the pan on low heat and add it to the pan to sweat them off.

2.Next, add your rosemary and mince to the pan, brown off the mince, and add your tomatoes, cayenne, mustard, and dark soy. Season to taste.

3.Then add your passata and cook for five minutes, followed by your beer and stock, and finally your milk and Scotch Bonnet.

4.Simmer on low to medium heat until the liquid has reduced by half.

5.Then bring your salted pasta water onto boil and add your pasta. Cook for 3 minutes.

6.Then save half a cup of the pasta water aside. Using tongs, add your fresh pasta to the bolognese with your chopped parsley and roll through until it is completely coated.

7.Take it off the heat, plate it up, and make it as cheesy as my jokes haha!! Enjoy guys!!

SHAKSHUKA

 2-4 servings 🕓 35 minutes

Steps for Cooking:

1.Heat 2 tsp of olive oil in a skillet or deep-based frying pan on medium heat before adding your onions, garlic, and peppers and sweat them down until softened (about 6 minutes). We do not want to add colour just soften the ingredients, so keep stirring and reduce the heat if you start to see browning.

2.Next, preheat your oven to Gas mark 5 and add your powder spices and chilli flake then mince or meat to the mix in your pan. If using fresh mince brown the meat off, or if you're using precooked, mix through until fully incorporated and warmed through before adding your harissa paste, fresh and tinned tomatoes and fresh kale, and cook for around 10 minutes or until the sauce has thickened.

3.Next, take your pan off the heat and make 4 wells in the sauce (holes where you can crack an egg into), then carefully crack an egg into each well, being mindful not to break the yolk (cracking the egg on a completely flat surface will help this process, I hope haha) then return the pan to a really low heat and cover with a lid to cook the eggs (keep checking on them if your lid is not see-through as you want the whites' to be set but the egg to be runny this should take around 6 minutes).

4.While your eggs are cooking in the sauce, cut your bread into rustic chunks, drizzle with the rest of the olive oil, and season with salt and pepper. Get them on a tray and in the oven until golden brown.

5.Take your pan off the heat, season the eggs, finish with your fresh coriander, crumbled feta (if using), and beautifully toasted bread, and go in for that yolk break.

Notes

Breakfast should be sooner, if you're making a Shakshuka. Enjoy!!

Ingredients:

1 Tin Diced Tomatoes
350g Ground Minced Beef/Lamb or Pre Cooked Meat from a Joint from the night before or Soya Mince for Vegetarian Version
5 tbsp Olive Oil
1 Red Onion (Sliced)
3 Medium Vine Ripened Tomatoes (Diced)
2 Cloves Minced Garlic
1tsp Smoked Paprika
1tsp Harissa Paste
1 tsp Red Chillli Flake
1 tsp Ground Cumin
1 tsp Ground Coriander
4-6 Sweet Mini Peppers
A Handful of Freshly Chopped Kale
A Handful of Freshly Chopped Coriander
4 Large Free Range Eggs
Feta Cheese for Garnish (Optional)
1 Loaf of fresh Bloomer/Tiger Bread

FLYING STEAK NOODLES

 2-4 servings   45 minutes

Ingredients:

2 Ribeye Steaks
1 Packet (5 nests) Instant Egg Noodles
Vegetable Oil for Frying
2 Large Eggs
1 tsp Chilli Flakes
2 tbsp Sesame Oil
500ml Beef Broth/Stock
Spring Onions
1 Red Onion

1 Clove Garlic
1 tsp Sesame Seeds
1 tbsp Dark Soy
1 tbsp White Vinegar
1 tbsp Chinese 5 Spice
2 tbsp Butter
2tbsp Olive Oil
1 Bunch Fresh Coriander
Salt and Pepper to taste

You will need some chopsticks and steel ladle for this to work.

Steps for Cooking:

1.Ensure that your steaks are out of the fridge and have been brought down to room temperature (this should take about 30 minutes after removing them from the fridge). Rub the steaks in the sesame oil and season generously with salt and pepper (it's always better to have extra seasoning when it comes to steak as you will lose 30 percent of it in the pan). Set aside.

2.Next, get your water on to boil for your noodles as per packet instructions (usually they say bring a pan of salted water to a rolling boil, drop your nests in so they are covered in the water, then take the pan off the heat and cover with a lid for 5 minutes, giving the noodles an occasional stir so they don't stick). While your noodles are in the water, get your vegetable oil in a deep pot and fill it a quarter of the way up and get it on a low/medium heat.

3.Next, you want to drain your noodles in a colander, then get them straight onto some paper towel and dab them until they're totally dry (remember, oil and water do not mix, so this part is crucial). Once your noodles are dry, get your chopsticks and wrap a couple of the noodles around the thin ends of the chopsticks to hold them together. Then, once they are secure, get the rest of the noodles and using the same process, wrap them around the chopsticks to give the effect that you are picking up the whole lot with the chopsticks.

4.Now, this is the tricky part. Your oil should be hot by now, so carefully lower the noodles on the chopsticks into the oil. You only want the oil to cover just under a quarter of the noodles from the bottom. Bob the noodles up and down carefully while keeping the bottom submerged in the oil, as this is how you will create a base for the noodles to stand on.

.Next, get your ladle and carefully spoon the hot oil over the rest of the noodles, working from the top and allowing the oil to run down the noodles, which will in effect fry and harden them around the chopsticks. It will take time, so be patient and test the strength of the noodles against the chopsticks to ensure they don't break.

.When you are comfortable that the noodles are hard and the chopsticks are secure, lift the noodles carefully out of the pan and straight onto some paper towel to drain.

.Next, get your spring onion, coriander, and garlic finely chopped and your red onion finely sliced, and soften your butter before mixing in the Chinese five spice and a sprinkle of coriander. Get a saucepan of water to a boil with your white vinegar on low heat for your eggs.

.Next, get a frying pan on a medium/high heat and have your steaks to hand. Once the pan begins to smoke, add your olive oil and lay your steaks away from you so you don't get hot oil splashes.

.Now Ribeye steak is a very flavourful cut with plenty of marbling (fat inside the muscle of the steak), so it doesn't take long and is very easy to overcook. Ideally, you want to cook them for 1 minute, then flip and cook for another minute, then add your Chinese five spice butter to the pan and baste the steaks, flipping them at 30-second intervals, until your total cooking time for both steaks is 4 and a half minutes for a perfect medium rare (if you have a meat thermometer, you are looking for around 54 degrees internal temperature).

0.Remove your steaks and rest on a wooden board covered loosely with tin foil (resting keeps the juices in the meat, which means when you slice it, it will be delicious and succulent; normally, kitchen rules say to rest your steak for as long as you have cooked it for, but but a few extra minutes is more beneficial than not). DO NOT PUT YOUR STEAK PAN IN THE SINK OR WASH IT. ALL THAT STUFF AT THE BOTTOM IS PURE FLAVOUR.

11.Next, get your eggs cracked singularly into individual cups or ramekins so the yolks stay in tact and keep to one side. Get your steak pan back on the heat and add a splash of oil if needed. Add your red onions and garlic and start to caramelise them (colouring the onions using their own natural sweetness). Once they start to brown, get your soy sauce in, give them a mix, and add your beef broth or stock to the pan. Turn the heat right down and let that simmer away nicely.

12.Now, check the water for your eggs; it will be fully warmed through. Give it a top-up with some boiled water from the kettle if needed, and crank the heat up once you've got it all boiling. Turn the heat down to medium, swirl the water around using a whisk to create a vortex, and drop your eggs in carefully, one at a time.

13.Get a bit of paper towel down on a flat plate or surface, and once your eggs have set (2 and a half to 3 minutes; you have to be like a hawk watching these; the minute the whites firm up, get them out) using a slotted spoon , remove them from the water and straight onto the paper towel to drain.

14.Now the fun part: we are ready to plate! Carefully move your fried noodles onto a plate; you want the base to be comfortable towards the centre. Next, get your steak sliced into nice, even strips and place them to the right of the base of the noodles, then season your eggs on the paper towel with the chilli flake and a pinch of salt and pepper and place them towards the front of the base. Pour your delicious beef broth over the steak and noodles, give the eggs a quick poke for their gorgeous yolks, and finish off with a sprinkling of your sesame seeds, fresh coriander, and spring onions.

You have just officially made noodles fly! Enjoy!!

Ingredients:

8 Medium/6 Large Red
Onions
1 Can of Guinness Irish Stout
2 Cloves of Minced Garlic
½ tsp Cayenne Pepper
(Optional)
5 tbsp Olive Oil
2 tbsp Butter
1 tsp Sugar
1 Litre Good Quality
Beef/Chicken or Vegetable
Stock
2 Sprigs of Thyme
1 Sprig of Rosemary
2 Bay Leaves
French Baugette or Crusty
Bread/Rolls
Gruyere or Mozarelle Cheese
Grated Parmesan
Fresh Chives
Salt and Pepper to Taste

GUINNESS FRENCH ONION SOUP

 2-4 servings   🕐 1 hour and 10 minutes

Steps for Cooking:

1.Peel your onions and get them sliced as thinly as possible using a sharp knife, then in a deep saucepan heat half your oil over medium heat and add your onions and coat them in the oil. Cook them down until they have softened (about 10–15 minutes).

2.Then, increase the heat to medium-high, add the rest of your oil and butter to the pan, and caramelise your onions for around 30 minutes, stirring often, until they are beautifully browned. Then add your sugar (this helps the caramelisation while enhancing the natural sweetness of the onion) and cook for another 10 minutes before adding your minced garlic, cayenne pepper (if using), and season well with salt and pepper.

3.Next, deglaze the pan by adding the Guinness to the pan and scraping any brown or sticky bits at the bottom and sides of the pan back into the onion mix (colour means flavour). Then, add in your stock, bay leaves, rosemary, and thyme; cover with a lid; and simmer on low heat for a further 30 minutes.

4.While your soup is simmering, cut your bread into even pieces and brush with a bit of olive oil on both sides before placing them on a baking tray and putting them in the grill to lightly toast on gas mark 5 for about 5 minutes. Take them out and sprinkle individually with your gruyere or mozzarella before returning them back to the oven until the cheese is bubbling and lightly browned.

5.Finally, take your soup off the heat, season with salt and pepper if needed, and ladle it into soup bowls, topping each bowl with a bit of cheesy toast, a dusting of parmesan, and some fresh chives.

Notes

What's the best thing about this recipe? ...... Guinness comes in packs of 4, so you get to drink the other 3. Enjoy!!

FOUR CHEESE MAC AND CHEESE

 2-4 servings  1 hour

Steps for Cooking:

1.Boil your pasta in fresh water with plenty of salt (salting water stops the pasta from sticking and helps to release some of the starch). Boil until al dente (about 3 minutes, or as your packet states) and set aside.

2.Dice your gammon chop with the fat incorporated and add to a cold pan with no oil (adding to a cold pan will help the fat render, which is where the flavour will come from) and colour until cooked and crisp.

3.Set the gammon aside, and in the same pan, add your butter on a low heat until fully melted (it's important that the heat is low as we do not want to brown the butter). Once melted, add your flour slowly while mixing consistently until you get a breadcrumb-type texture. Cook the flour out (your flour mix will be nut brown by now and the kitchen will smell of biscuits, once that happens, slowly add your cream, then your milk a bit at a time, working out any lumps until you're left with a smooth velvety sauce, then add your turmeric and mustard (taste and season accordingly; if you can still taste raw flour, it isn't ready yet).

4.Next, add your cheeses (again, a bit at a time, working out the lumps before adding more so you keep the consistency before adding the gammon back into the pan).

5.Finally, once the sauce is complete, add the pasta back into the pan, mix it into the sauce until it is fully coated, sprinkle your fresh chopped parsley in, and give it a final mix.

6.Finally, leave it to sit for 10 minutes so the sauce can thicken and set slightly. Sprinkle over some more mozzarella and Emmental (to get the cheese pull). Finish with your panko breadcrumbs and get it in the oven the oven gas mark 5 for 12 minutes or until golden brown like me haha!! Enjoy guys!

Ingredients:

VEGETARIAN OPTION FRIENDLY

500g Tube Pasta
1 Fatty Gammmon Chop, or Unsmoked Bacon Lardons
Half a Cup of Double Cream
500ml Whole Milk
50g Unsalted Butter
50g Plain Flour
Fresh Chopped Parsley
Seasoned Panko Breadcrumbs
4 cheeses (I used Sharp Cheddar, Emmental, Red Leicester and Mozzarella)
Half tbsp of Turmeric
Half a tbsp of Coarse Grain Mustard
Salt and Pepper to taste

(The Cheese and Gammon will already be salty so taste as you go.)

POSH CHICKEN NUGGETS AND CHIPS

 2-4 servings   45 minutes

Ingredients:

For the Nuggets:
2 Large Chicken Breasts
1 Diced Onion
1 Chicken Stock Cube
Salt
Pepper
½ tsp Smoked Paprika
½ tsp Mild Curry Powder
½ tsp Dried Oregano
½ tsp Garlic Powder

For the Batter:
Dry Plain Flour for
Dusting (Seasoned)
350g Plain Flour
150g Corn Flour
2 Eggs
½ tsp Turmeric
Cold Sparkling Water
Salt
Pepper

For the Ketchup:
8 Tomatoes
1 Clove of Minced Garlic
2 Finely Diced Onions
1 tbsp Oilve Oil
1 tbsp White Vinegar
½ tsp Chilli Flake
(optional)
½ tsp Sugar
Salt and Pepper to taste

For the Chips:
3 Large Maris Piper
Potatoes
Oil for Deep Frying

Steps for Cooking:

1. Preheat your oven to Gas mark 1, then get all of your ketchup ingredients onto a tray. Drizzle over the oil and vinegar then evenly sprinkle your sugar, salt and pepper and chilli flake if using.

2.Allow the ingredients to sit for an hour and a half in the oven to get rid of as much moisture as possible. Remove from the oven, blitz the ingredients in a blender, then press the sauce using a spoon or spatula through a sieve, and allow to cool.

3.Peel your potatoes and cut them into thick chips before rinsing and soaking in cold salted water for 30 minutes (soaking the chips in cold salted water allows the excess starch to be removed, which makes for a crispier chip).

4.While the chips are soaking, you can make your nugget batter by whisking together your plain and corn flours with the other ingredients. Add your sparkling water a bit at a time until you have a smooth batter. Cover it in cling film and pop it in the fridge until later.

5.Next, get a pan of salted water on the gas on medium/high heat. Drain your chips and give them a dab with a paper towel to remove any additional starch. Pop them into your salted water and blanch (blanching basically helps to keep the inside of the potato soft and fluffy, like a pillow of potatoey goodness). You want the

hips to be just be just reaching fork tender before you remove them, drain them in a colander, and get them on a baking tray lined with parchment paper, then into the fridge (minimum 0 minutes, maximum overnight).

.Next, for the nugget mix, get all of the chicken nugget ingredients into a blender and, using your pulse setting, break the ingredients down until you have a rustic paste. Flour your work surface, scrape the mix out onto the surface, and form into large nugget shapes and get them on a tray.

.Next, add your frying oil to a deep saucepan vegetable or sunflower is perfect) and get it on medium heat. Get your seasoned dusting flour ready along with your batter (to check your oil, drop a tiny bit of batter into the oil; if it sizzles and puffs up to the top, your oil's good to go). Then, one at a time, dredge your nuggets into the flour, shake off all of the excess, then dip them into your batter to ensure it is fully coated (the flour helps the batterstick), then straight into the oil, frying in batches of 3–4 to not overcrowd the pan.

.As you fry your nuggets, set up some paper towels on a tray for them to drain on and get your chips out of the fridge. Once the nuggets are all fried, drain them on the paper towel, cover them loosely in foil, and get them in your preheated oven to keep warm.

.Next, while the oil is still on medium heat, add your chips and fry until just below golden brown, then remove them onto a tray to drain. Turn your heat up to high and add the chips back into the oil carefully for a second fry. This will add a different level of crunch to the outer layer while the inside remains fluffy due to the blanching process. fry until golden brown, then remove onto your draining tray and season with salt.

0.Get your plate/board, or your chosen food vessel ready (for these nuggets, I'd be happy with a trough full of them haha) add your ketchup to a small bowl or ramekin , get your nuggets out of the oven, and arrange them beautifully along with your chunky triple-cooked chips.

McDonald's meets Michelin!
Enjoy guys!!

DOUBLE BONE MARROW BURGER

 2-4 servings

 45 minutes

Ingredients:

For the Patties:
500g Good Quality Beef Mince
15-20% Fat
1 tbsp Panko Breadcrumbs
1 Egg
Bone Marrow
1 tsp Chilli Powder
1 tsp Garlic Powder
1 tsp Dried Rosemary
1 tsp Dried Thyme
1 tsp Garlic Powder
1 tsp Onion Powder
1 tsp Smoked Paprika
1 Crumbled Beef Stock Cube
Salt and Pepper to taste

For the Burger Sauce:
250ml Mayonnaise
250ml Ketchup
150ml American Style Mustard
4 Small Sweet Gherkins
1 tsp White Vinegar
Splash of Gherkin Jar Brine
1 tsp Onion Powder
1 tsp Smoked Paprika
Sprinkling of Freshly Chopped Parsley

Additional Ingredients:
Beef Marrow Bones, Emmental Cheese (Sliced), Sliced Red Onion, Shredded Iceberg Lettuce, Olive Oil, Extra Gherkins, Brioche Bun

Steps for Cooking:

1. Pre-heat your oven to Gas Mark 8 and season your marrow bones with a little olive oil, sea salt, and cracked black pepper. This has to be done in two stages, so you will cook the first bone individually for around 15 minutes or until the marrow starts to bubble (do not overcook the marrow or it will completely liquify).

2. Once cooked, set aside and add all of your burger ingredients to a bowl, incorporating everything. Carefully scoop out the bone marrow and add it to your burger mix as well, and form into patties.

3. Next, get all of your burger sauce ingredients into a bowl, give them a good mix, and pop them in the fridge until later.

4. Then, get your second marrow bone in your pre-heated oven and get a skillet or good-quality frying pan on medium to high heat. As soon as the pan starts to smoke, add your patties to the pan (cook them for around 2 and a half minutes per side for a good crust and medium rare middle). Once the first side is cooked, flip the patties and add the cheese on top and the onions around the burger. Add a bit of water to the pan, then cover the burgers with a bowl. This will create steam to keep the burgers nice and moist and help the cheese melt.

5. Take your burgers out of the pan once the cheese has melted, smother both patties with the onions, and set aside covered with a bit of tin foil to rest. Then remove your bone marrow from the oven.

6. Using the same pan you cooked the burgers in, toast your brioche bun, wiping the bun around the burger juices to soak up all of the residual flavour. Once they are golden brown, we are ready to build.

7. Now, we start with the base of the bun, then, using a spoon, spread some of your burger sauce on the lettuce, then your first patty covered in that gooey cheese and those delicious caramelised onions, then some more lettuce, then the second patty, cover the inside of your top bun with some more of that burger sauce, and then top your burger off, get it on a board with your full bone marrow, and voila!

Notes

There's no need to be hungry any further, because you've got yourself a Double Bone Marrow Burger. Enjoy!

BOXING DAY BUBBLE AND SQUEAK

2-4 servings 🕐 30 minutes

Ingredients:

1 tsp Duck Fat/Butter
1 Onion (Diced)
1 Clove of Garlic (Diced)
150g of Unsmoked Bacon Lardons
300g Cold Leftover Cabbage, Sprouts and Potatoes (or you could use Fresh Cabbage and Mashed/Crushed Potatoes)

½ tsp Cayenne Pepper
½ tsp Smoked Paprika
Pinch of Chilli Flake
1 Large Free Range Egg
1 tsp White Vinegar
Salt and Pepper to taste

Steps for Cooking:

Firstly, get a small saucepan full of water with your white vinegar in it and put it on a low simmer. This will be for your egg.

Next, preheat your oven to Gas Mark 4, then in a cold, deep-based frying pan, add your lardons directly to the pan, then add your pan to a low or medium heat (putting the lardons directly into a cold pan allows the fat to render or melt).

Once your lardons have begun to cook and brown slightly, add in your duck fat or butter and your onion and garlic. Continue to cook until your onions have coloured slightly. Season with salt and pepper and your paprika and cayenne.

Next, add your cabbage and sprouts to the pan and mix thoroughly. Allow the cabbage to colour in the pan; this should take between 5-8 minutes.

Next, add your cold mash/potatoes to the pan and work them through the mixture, pushing and compressing everything down in the pan to form the shape and set as it cooks and forms a crust.

Increase the heat of your boiling water to get it to a rolling boil while keeping an eye on your Bubble and Squeak. Lift it lightly with a fish slice and check the underside. If it is browned beautifully, you are ready to flip it to achieve the same colour on the other side. Then, put the pan straight into your preheated oven, loosely covered with some tin foil.

7.Next, you want to achieve a perfectly rounded poached egg, so crack your egg directly into a fine sieve to get rid of the stringy bits of white, turn the heat down from a rolling boil to a medium simmer in your water, add a pinch of salt to the water, and whisk it gently to create a weak vortex (a couple of stirs just to move the water around), then carefully drop your egg into the water directly from the sieve and poach until the white has perfectly encased the yolk and set.

8.Remove your poached egg from the water using a slotted spoon and get it directly onto a plate with some paper towel to drain the excess water. Season with a pinch of salt and pepper and some chilli flake if you wish.

9.Carefully take your Bubble and Squeak out of the oven using an oven glove, as the handle will be red hot, and using a fish slice, slide it onto a wooden board. You can be as creative as you like with the presentation of this dish because it is very giving in terms of the textures, flavours and simplicity of it.

Notes

This is the ultimate boxing day hangover cure, so don't worry if you let the bubbles go to your head over the festive period; this squeak will fix your whole week. Enjoy!!

TANDOORI CHICKEN TIKKA MASALA WITH GARLIC AND CUMIN FLATBREAD

 2-4 servings   1 hour and 30 minutes

Ingredients:

For the Chicken Marinade:
1kg Diced Chicken Breast in Big Chunks
500ml Plain Yoghurt
2 tsbp Minced Garlic and Ginger Paste
1 tbsp Garam Masala
1 tsp Ground Cumin
1 tsp Kashmiri chilli (or extra hot Red chilli Powder
1 tbsp Red Food Colouring
Chopped Coriander Stalks
The Zest and Juice of one Lemon
2 Thick Fresh Green Chillies Chopped into Thick Slices

For the Sauce:
1 tsp Coriander Seeds
1 tsp Mustard Seeds
1 tsp Whole Cumin Seeds
1 Star Anise
1 Stick Cinnamon
3 tbsp Olive Oil
1 Large Onion (2 Small) Diced
2 tbsp Minced Garlic and Ginger Paste
2 tsp Garam Masala
2 tsp Ground Cumin
2 tsp Turmeric Powder
2 tsp Ground Coriander
1 tsp Red Chilli Powder
500 ml To Good Quality Chicken Stock
2 tbsp Creme Fraiche with a dash milk to give you a sauce like texture
500ml of passata (or a couple of tins of chopped tomatoes blitzed)

For the Flatbreads:
300g Self Raising Flour
1 tsp Baking Powder
150g Natural Yoghurt
1 tbsp Olive Oil
1 tsp Cumin Seeds
1 tsp Grated Garlic
1 tsp Nigella Seeds
1 tbsp Honey
1 Egg
Melted Butter with Chopped Garlic and Coriander for Brushing
1 Fresh Chopped Green chilli for Garnish

Steps for Cooking:

1.Get your chicken in a bowl and add the marinade ingredients, starting with the powdered spices, then adding the rest. Mix thoroughly so the chicken is completely coated, and pop back in the fridge to marinate (minimum 2 hours, maximum overnight).

2.Once marinated, remove your chicken from the fridge 20 minutes before cooking to bring it down to room temperature (bringing it down to room temperature ensures even cooking), then using a skillet or deep-based frying pan, get it on medium/high heat, and just as it begins to smoke, add 2 tablespoons of olive oil and place your chicken chunks into the pan (move them around the oil as you place them so the yoghurt doesn't stick).

3.Once placed, allow the chicken to cook until it slowly releases from the pan. Avoid moving it around once it's placed, as you want that charred effect for both colour and flavour. After 5 minutes, check the underside of the pieces, and if you have a nice even char, they're ready to flip and do the exact same thing on the other side.

4.Next, once your chicken is charred, remove it from the pan and set it aside (do not wash or clean the pan; all of those sticky and charred bits are full of flavour and the base for your sauce). Then you want to add your dry spices to that pan on very low heat to toast them (star anise, coriander seeds, cumin seeds, and cinnamon stick. Toasting your spices first will activate them and enhance their flavour). Once you can smell the spices in the air, add the remaining olive oil to the pan and your onion. Allow the onion to caramelise on a low heat for 10–15 minutes.

5.Next, add your garlic and ginger paste to the pan along with your powder spices, then deglaze the pan with your chicken stock, scraping all of the sticky bits at the bottom of the pan and incorporating them back into the mix. Add in your passata and allow the sauce to simmer for 15 minutes. Season to taste, then take the pan off the heat and allow the sauce to cool completely.

6.While the sauce is cooling, let's get started on these flatbreads. So, in a bowl, combine your flour, baking powder, and yoghurt with a pinch of salt and a drizzle of water and work into a rustic dough.

7.Once your dough is formed, add your garlic, seeds, honey, and crack an egg into the mix and massage the ingredients through the dough to bring them together (the honey will add a delicious sweetness to the bread, whilst the egg will give you that takeaway naan-style crunch). Cover your dough and set it aside.

8.Once your sauce has completely cooled, remove the cinnamon stick and star anise as they have served their purpose in terms of flavour, then carefully pour the sauce into a blender and blitz until perfectly smooth. Get your pan back on the heat on the lowest possible heat and add your sauce back into the pan along with your chicken and simmer.

9.Next, get another heavy-based saucepan on high heat and roll your dough using your hands into balls on a floured surface. Roll each ball into a flat bread shape, getting them as thin as possible without tearing. Cook in your hot pan for 1-2 minutes on either side. Repeat this process until all of your flatbreads are cooked.

10. Get your butter in a bowl and blast it through the microwave for 20 seconds on high heat or until the butter is completely melted. Add your chopped coriander and garlic to the melted butter and brush your flatbreads generously.

11.Turn the flame up on your chicken to give it a final blast of heat, adjust any seasoning to your taste, then give it a good squeeze of lemon over the top to wake all of the flavours back up again and give it a good mix. Take it off the heat and spoon over your creme fraiche sauce to get it looking nice and pretty, then finish with some fresh coriander and chopped green chilli.

Notes

Trust me guys, when it comes to a curry... this one tikka's all the boxes. Enjoy!!

THE HUMBLE POTATO

Well, what can I say? It's the staple of any substantial dish and arguably one of the most diverse ingredients in cookery across the world.

So for those reasons (plus, like a potato, I am also brown and round) I thought it would only be right to dedicate a section purely to the most popular variations of everyone's favourite starchy vegetable.

CHIPS

It wouldn't be a potato section without the famous chip. Crunchy, fluffy, and absolutely delicious. The secret to getting the perfect chip is frying them in good-quality oil, soaking them in cold water for at least 30 minutes once peeled to remove the excess starch, blanching them to keep that middle nice and fluffy, and then cooling them in the fridge to help with that crunchy exterior when you fry.

ROAST POTATO

Another classic variation that we all know and love, the roast potato, is no stranger to any British kitchen on a

Sunday and with so many different ways to tweak them it's no wonder why they are so loved. My go -to recipe is to boil the potatoes in water with a beef stock cube (or veg stock for the vegetarian option), some fresh rosemary, and fresh thyme until fork tender. Carefully take the potatoes out using a slotted spoon (save the stock for soup or gravy if you're doing a roast) and ruffle in a colander and pop them on the side to cool while you heat up a baking dish with beef dripping/olive oil fresh rosemary/fresh thyme and a whole bulb of garlic chopped in half. Get it nice and hot in the oven (gas mark 6), then take it out, coat your potatoes, and get them back in for 35 minutes, turning regularly, until evenly golden brown and crunchy...nom nom!

MASHED POTATO

Another classic in the Winter Warmer category, there's so many ways to mash a potato!!!!! I'm sure you all have your go-too version of this classic accompaniment. My go-to version is boil your diced potatoes in salted water get them drained once they're cooked, and then back into the same saucepan. Add a raw egg yolk (adds richness to the mash as well as colour if using it as a topping to go back in the oven) plenty of salt and pepper, a good knob of butter, a teaspoon of french mustard, a sprinkling of fresh parsley, and a good glug of milk. Get it all mashed up, and that will go with anything.

THE HUMBLE POTATO

guilty pleasures. My go-to recipe is to finely dice your potato and get it in a frying pan on low heat. You do not want to colour the potato; only cook it about half way. Once the potato starts to slightly soften, get it into a bowl and mix with flour, cornflour, your choice of spices, and a grated onion with all of the moisture removed. Get your potato mix onto some baking paper, form it into a hash brown shape, and pop it in the freezer for half an hour to set in shape. Heat some good-quality oil, get your hash brown in, and fry until golden brown... Well Done.. Ronald Mcdonald would be proud!

FONDANT POTATO

hese little bundles of potatoey joy are the ones to pull ut when you're trying to impress—the perfect way to levate your plate to a five-star delight. Shape your otatoes (either square or round, as long as they're even) nd olive oil to a deep-based skillet or saucepan. Once ne oil is hot get your potatoes in and colour on one side, nce coloured flip them over and begin to colour the ther side while adding butter, garlic, fresh rosemary, and resh thyme to the pan, basting the potatoes as you go. hen add in some good-quality chicken stock filling the an to three-quarters of the way up the potatoes, being areful not to cover them in the liquid and get them in a reheated oven at gas mark 5 for 30 minutes or until ender.

JACKET POTATO

I could go on all day about the different ways to cook a potato, but finally, on our jacket-based journey, I thought I would leave you with one of my variations that you will either agree with or you won't ... Does gravy belong on a jacket potato with beans? I'll let you decide.

HASH BROWN

Well, it's not full English without a couple of these bad boys, is it? Crunchy, Fluffy, and Moreish—these really are

"FAKE" STEAK N ALE PIE DINNER

 2-4 servings   1 hour and 45 minutes

VEGETARIAN OPTION FRIENDLY

Ingredients:

For the Pies:
500g Quorn "Steak" Strips
2 Packs of Jus Roll Vegan Puff Pastry
1 Onion Finely Diced
2 Cloves of Garlic Finely Diced
1 Sprig of Rosemary
1 Sprig of Thyme
2 Bay Leaves
1 Stick Celery Finely Diced
1 Carrot Finely Doced
½ Cup Frozen Peas
Handful of Sliced Button Mushrooms
1 tbsp Olive Oil
1 tbsp Dark Soy
½ tsp Cayenne Pepper
1 Vegetable Stock Cube
1 tsp Brown Sugar
300ml Dark Ale
Salt and Pepper to Taste

For the Carrots:
4 Carrots Peeled and Chopped evenly
2 tbsp Honey
2 tbsp Olive Oil
2 tbsp Butter
1 tsp chilli Flake

For the Cauliflower Cheese:
1/2 A Large Cauliflower broken into
Florets
Bechamel Sauce (follow the recipe
for Bechamel in my lasagne recipe in
this book)
½ tsp Cayenne Pepper
200g Grated Cheddar
150g Grated Gruyere/Emmental
½ tsp Turmeric
Panko Breadcrumbs
2 tbsp Olive Oil

For the Potatoes:
6 Maris Pepper Potatoes peeled and
cut on the angle
4 Sprigs Fresh Rosemary
4 Sprigs Fresh Thyme
1 Bulb of Garlic Chopped in Half
1 Vegetable Stock Cube
250ml Olive Oil

For the Gravy:
Potato Stock Water
1 Small Onion Finely Diced
1 tbsp Dark Soy
Leftover Ale (is that even a thing? ⬤)
Extra Vegetable Stock Cube (if needed)
Salt and Pepper to Tatse

Steps for Cooking:

1.Pre-heat your oven to Gas Mark 6, get your cauliflower on a tray seasoned with your olive oil, salt, and pepper, and roast in the oven for 40 minutes. Next, grease 2 large foil pie cases and line with your puff pastry (you can shape the pastry using a bowl and a knife if you don't have pastry cutters; just ensure that the whole of the base and sides of the foil are covered and you leave enough pastry for the lid).

2.Next, get your oil in a pan and on medium heat, fry off your onion, garlic, carrot, and celery until softened, then get your "steak" in (you can add a bit more oil if you wish), then add the rest of your pie mix ingredients, starting with the mushrooms, then your peas, and finish with your crumbled stock cube. Top off with your ale and reduce for 15 minutes (reducing means cooking down so the liquid evaporates, which means the flavour of the ingredients in the pan is more intense. You want the mix to have a thick saucey consistency, so once it's reduced, feel free to add some more ale or a splash of water if needed, just remember to adjust the seasoning accordingly as well).

3.Next, remove the rosemary, thyme, and bay leaves from the mix and pour the mixture evenly into the pie cases, before topping off with the excess pastry as a lid and crimping around the pie using a fork or the handle end of a metal ladle (the little rounded shape at the end of most metal utensils can be used to

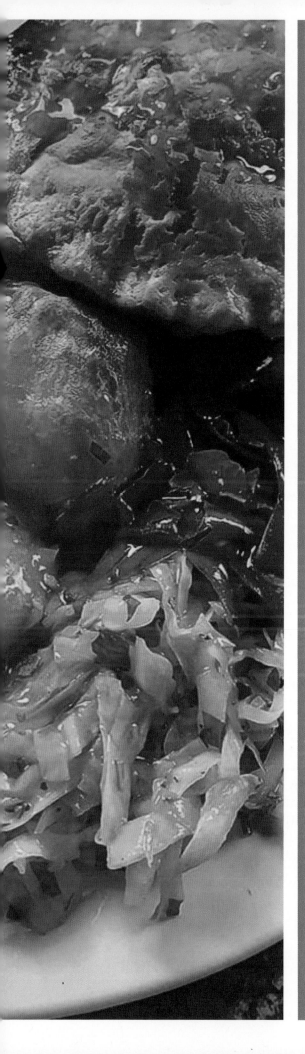

press around your pie to make a nice pattern). Set the pies aside and cover loosely with a clean tea towel and get your cauliflower out of the oven.

4.Next, get a saucepan of water to a boil and add in half your rosemary, thyme, and stock cube until it is completely dissolved and the water has come to a boil. Then, get your potatoes in and boil until fork tender, then take them out using a slotted spoon (do not discard the water as this will be gravy). Ruffle the potatoes in a colander and set aside to cool.

5.In a deep baking tray, add your oil and the rest of your rosemary and thyme, along with your garlic, and get it in the oven to heat up. You want it to be smoking hot, which will help create a crust around your potatoes. Start your milk for your bechamel while the oil heats.

6.Next, get your oil out and carefully add your potatoes into the oil, rolling them using a spoon to ensure that they are fully coated, then get them back in the oven along with your pies for 45 minutes (check your pies regularly and turn your potatoes each time to ensure an even colour).

7.Now, get your cauliflower in your serving dishes and finish off your bechamel, adding in your cayenne, turmeric, and mustard directly to the sauce once you've taken it off the heat. Spoon over the roasted cauliflower and top with your panko and your cheeses, then get them in the oven as well.

8.Next, get a small saucepan on medium heat, add in 2 tbsp of oil and 2 tbsp of butter, and get your carrots in colouring them on all sides before adding in your honey (if you don't have a squeezy honey bottle, dip your spoon in olive oil and let the excess drip off before wiping with a paper towel, then use that spoon to get your honey out of the jar so it won't stick to the spoon and make a mess). Gently glaze the carrots and turn the heat down to low/medium. Add a ladle of water and cover with a lid to allow the carrots to steam for 10 minutes before removing the lid and finishing in the oven.

9.At this stage, keep an eye on things to ensure that nothing is overcooked. Feel free to turn the heat down slightly if you are slightly behind. Don't worry, it's all part of the fun; we're nearly there now.

10.For your gravy, get some oil in a pan and fry your onion on medium heat until caramelised then add your potato water (the starch from the potatoes will act as a thickener) into the pan followed by your dark soy and the rest of your ale, and reduce down until you reach your desired consistency (again, balance the seasoning with a bit of brown sugar if the ale makes the gravy a bit too bitter or a bit of extra vegetable stock). Keep warm on low heat.

11.Now, you're ready to plate, let your creativity flow, use a bit of extra vegetables on the side if you like, and let the colours complement each other; it's your dish, own it.

Notes

Before making this dish , I never knew fake steak was an actual thing..... I thought they were steakin' the piss!

Enjoy guys!!

ROASTED BAINGAN MASALA

 2-4 servings

 1 hour

Ingredients:

6-8 Small Aubergines
2 tbsp Ginger Garlic Paste
2 Red Onions Diced
4 Fresh Birdseye chillis Finely Chopped
2 tbsp Fresh Coriander Stalks Finely Chopped
Handful of Fresh Cherry Tomatoes Diced
3 tbsp Olive Oil

Dry Spices:
1 tbsp Coriander Seeds
1 tsp Cumin Seeds
1 Cinnamon Stick
1 Star Anise
1 Bay Lef

Powdered Spices:
1 tsp Coriander Powder
2 tsp chilli Powder
2 tsp Garam Masala
1 tsp Turmeric
3 tsp Salt

200ml Coconut Milk
150ml Passata
150ml Vegetable Stock
1 tsp Tomato Sauce
Fresh Coriander Leaves
Creme Fraiche with a dash of Milk (Sauce like consistency for Garnish

Steps for Cooking:

1. Preheat your oven to Gas Mark 4. Cut a cross shape in the bottom of each aubergine about half an inch thick (this will help the vegetable release any excess water during roasting). Season your aubergine with 1 tbsp of olive oil, 1 tsp of salt, 1 tsp of chilli powder, and 1 tsp garam masala, massaging the seasoning into the skins (this will make them nice and crispy).

2. Next, heat a skillet or griddle pan until smoking hot, and add your aubergines to the pan, cooking them evenly until the skin gets nice and charred. Then, transfer your pan straight into the oven to let the aubergines cook through (10–12 minutes).

3. Next, in a separate pan, get it on a low heat and toast your dry spices (a low heat ensures they don't burn as they will become bitter at a high heat and spoil the dish). Toast them gently until you can smell the aroma, then get the rest of your olive oil in the pan along with your onions, green chillies, and coriander stalks. Turn the heat up to medium and cook the onions until they start to brown (your aubergine should be ready now, so get them out of the oven and cover loosely with some tin foil). Next, add your tomato puree, then your ginger garlic paste, then your fresh diced tomatoes, and cook for 5 minutes before adding your powdered spices. Then give everything a good mix before adding your stock, scraping up any bits that are at the bottom of the pan to add back into the sauce, then add your passata and simmer for 10 minutes before adding in your coconut milk and simmering for another 5 minutes.

4. Take out the star anise, the cinnamon stick, and the bay leaf from the sauce and discard them, then set your masala sauce aside until slightly cooled (while the sauce cools, get your creme fraiche in a bowl and mix it through with a dash of milk until you have a sauce-like consistency and get it in the fridge). Then get your cooled masala sauce in a blender and blitz until completely smooth.

5. Then add your masala sauce back into the pan on low heat and add your roasted aubergine to the sauce, adjusting your seasoning to taste. Once heated through, take your pan off the heat and stir through half of your fresh coriander leaves, then drizzle over your creme fraiche and finish with the rest of your coriander.

6. This dish goes beautifully with some basmati rice, or you can follow the garlic naan or flatbread recipes I have written in this book to share with you guys as well.

Notes

I remember doing the moonwalk after making this dish, then I realised.. Aubergine is not maaa lover, it's just a veg haha!
Enjoy guys!!

LASAGNE

🍴 2-4 servings　　🕐 1 hour

Steps for Cooking:

Begin your sauce by heating your oil in a deep pan and adding your mince and brown off, followed by your onion, carrot, and celery, and allowing it to cook until softened before adding your garlic, cayenne, and tomato puree. Season with salt and pepper.

Next, add in your tinned tomatoes, followed by the rest of your ragu ingredients, and finally the stock. Cover with a lid and gently simmer for an hour and a half.

Next for your bechamel, add your milk to a small saucepan, poke your cloves into the onion, and add it to the milk with your bayleaf. Bring it to the boil over a low/medium heat, then once it starts to boil, take it off the heat and let the onion and bayleaf sit in the milk for 15 minutes (this process is called infusing).

Now, in another saucepan, melt your butter until it begins to foam, then add your flour, salt, and pepper and cook over a low heat until you can no longer taste the flour (keep the heat as low as possible as you do not want to brown the mix; this should only take a couple of minute). Then add your infused milk in a bit at a time until you have a silky, smooth sauce (keep it warm over low heat).

Next, remove the rosemary, bay leaves, and thyme from your ragu and preheat your oven to Gas Mark 4. Now to assemble your lasagne, you want to add a ladle of sauce to the bottom of the dish, followed by your pasta sheets in one layer, then top the sheets with your bechamel and sprinkle over your cheddar and mozzarella. Repeat this process until your dish is filled, and finish the lasagne with a final layer of bechamel sauce and the rest of your cheddar and mozzarella. Bake for 35–45 minutes, or until the top is golden brown. Finish with your freshly grated parmesan and a sprinkling of fresh parsley, and serve with a lovely piece of fresh ciabatta or focaccia and some thyme-infused oil.

Notes

Make sure you have plenty of napkins handy with this lasagne, that way you'll get less on ya! Enjoy guys!

Ingredients:

For the Ragu:
250g Steak Mince
250g Pork Mince
Good Quality Beef Stock
2 tbsp Dark Soy
2 tbsp Tomato Puree
2 Tins Chopped Tomatoes
½ tsp Cayenne Pepper
1 Large Onion Finely Chopped
3 Cloves Minced Garlic
2 Sticks Celery Minced Garlic
1 Large Carrot Finely Diced
2 Sprigs Fresh Rosemary
2 Sprigs Fresh Thyme
2 Bay Leaves
100ml Whole Milk
1 tbsp Brown Sauce
1 tbsp Tomato Ketchup
2 tbsp Olive Oil

For the Bechamel Sauce:
500ml Whole Milk
50g Butter
50g Plain Flour
1 Small Onion (Peeled, Whole)
1 Bay Leaf
5 Cloves
Salt and Pepper to Tatse
Sprinkling of Freshly Chopped Parsley
Fresh Lasagne Sheets cut to the size of your lasagne dish
300g Cheddar
300g Mozzerella
250g Fresh Parmesan

TRIPLE CHOCOLATE BROWNIE WITH SPUN SALTED CARAMEL AND HOMEMADE CUSTARD RECIPE

 2-4 servings   30 minutes

VEGETARIAN OPTION FRIENDLY

Ingredients:

For the Brownie:
400g Milk Chocolate
200g White Chocolate
150 g Hersheys Peanut Butter Drops (you can use any combination of three types of Chocolate depending on you reference)
150g Unsalted Butter Diced
2 Free Range Eggs
175g Golden Caster Sugar
½ tsp Vanilla Essence
25g of 70% Cocoa Powder
100g Plain White Flour
2 tsp Baking Powder
Icing Sugar mixed with Cocoa Powder for Dusting

For the Spun Caramel:
250g Golden Caster Sugar
1 tsp Olive Oil
Pinch of Sea Salt

For the Custard:
350ml Whole Milk
2 Egg Yolks
25g Golden Caster Sugar
1 tsp Vanilla Essence

Steps for Cooking:

1. Preheat your oven to Gas mark 4 and line a deep square brownie/baking tray with baking paper (butter the tray first, and that will help the paper stick).

2. Next, melt half of your milk chocolate with your butter in a bain marie and gently whisk together (a bain marie is a small saucepan filled a quarter of the way up with water and put on low heat. Then, using a glass or ceramic bowl, put that into the saucepan, then your ingredients into the bowl so they melt via steam, not direct contact).

3. Once fully incorporated, take the bowl off the heat and set it aside. Whisk together your eggs and sugar until they have doubled in size, then, using a spatula, fold in your chocolate and butter mix. Folding gently instead of stirring will keep the air in the mix, which makes for a lighter brownie.

4. Now add the rest of your ingredients to the mix, leaving out the white chocolate, the rest of your milk chocolate, and the peanut butter drops. Put half of the mix in the tray, then arrange your chocolate pieces over that layer, then spoon over the rest of the mix to completely cover the chocolate pieces (this will give you a delicious gooey chocolate centre).

5. Get your brownie in the oven on the middle shelf; this will take around 30–35 minutes to bake.

Next, our spun caramel now gets a pint glass and turns upside down on a piece of foil (the foil is there to catch ay splashes, so fold it a couple of times to make sure s durable). With your pint glass still upside down, brush e base of the glass (which will now be the top) and a arter way up the sides with a thin layer of olive oil, wipe vay any excess with a paper towel.

Now keep your oiled glass close, get a saucepan on w-medium heat, and pour in your sugar, allowing it to ssolve fully (you can take it off the heat and mix it if you id it catching at the bottom of the pan), but the aim is to hieve a golden brown colour with the sugar completely ssolved, then add your salt. Now, get a spoon ready, id once the caramel starts to bubble, take it off the heat, ke a spoon of it, and hold the spoon above your glass, lowing the caramel to drip off the tip of the spoon while oving it quickly in different directions to give you a attern effect. Less is more at this stage, as the more you se, the thicker the pattern will be, so there's more iance of it setting as a big blob. So be sparing, as you in always do more after.

Now, allow the caramel to set around the base of your ass, and once you are confident that it's strong enough, owly slide the pattern off the glass (the oil you used arlier will help to make this a bit easier) and set the spun aramel aside somewhere where it won't get knocked.

Now your brownie should be done at this point, so move it from the oven. The best way to check is to get wooden skewer or cocktail stick and poke it into the entre of the brownie, and pull it out. If it has a wet ixture on it, then get it back in the oven, and if it comes ut near clean enough, then you're sorted. ●

0.Once cooked,get your brownie on a wire rack and let it ool down. Do not attempt to slice it straight away, or you ill end up with a gooey blob of chocolate. ●

11.While your brownie is cooling, it's custard time, so get your milk in a saucepan and set it to a low/medium heat, and add your vanilla essence. In a separate bowl, beat your eggs with your sugar using a wooden spoon rather than a whisk (normally, we use a fork or a whisk to beat eggs, but for custard, we want it thick so we don't want any air in the mix).

12.Then, slowly add your milk to the egg mixture, stirring carefully to make sure everything is fully incorporated, and you will be left with a smooth liquid. Next, pour the mixture into a pan on a very low heat (at this stage, if we add the mix to a high heat, you will be left with a bowl of sweet scrambled eggs, so temperature is key) and whisk until the liquid has thickened to your desired consistency. Take off the heat, pour the custard through a sieve into a bowl, and cover with foil.

13.Ideally, you would set your brownie in the fridge overnight to achieve the perfect consistency for cutting squares, but come on, who can resist that smell, especially after all that hard work? So as long as your brownie is cool enough cut yourself a square, give your custard a mix, and get it in a small ramekin. Dust the plate with your cocoa and icing sugar mix, and finish with your beautiful caramel decoration.

Notes

My ex asked me for a sweet chocolate brownie once.... I told her you've already got one.... Me... I think that's why she's my ex!

Enjoy!!

HONEY...I'M COMB!

 2-4 servings   10 minutes

Ingredients:

200g Caster Sugar
5 tbsp Golden Syrup

2 Drops of Vanilla Essence
1 tsp Bicarbonate of Soda

Steps for cooking:

1.Add your sugar, golden syrup, and vanilla essence to a clean, heavy-based saucepan. Get it on low heat and stir continuously with a wooden spoon or spatula until the mixture is completely dissolved. Do not allow it to bubble (once the sugar has dissolved, do not stir it again).

2.Now, turn the heat up to medium and heat the mixture until it reaches a lovely golden colour, then quickly take the pan off the heat, tip your bicarbonate of soda in, and whisk until the bicarb has completely disappeared and you're left with a beautiful, golden foaming mixture.

3.Pour the mixture into a deep baking tin lined with baking paper (you can butter the tin first to help the paper stick neatly) pouring as close to the base as possible so you don't lose any of the bubbles, and leave to cool before cracking into chunks.... Enjoy!!

POTTY ABOUT PANCAKES

 2-4 servings   15 minutes

Steps for Cooking:

1.Whisk together your flour, sugar, and baking soda in a large bowl, then in a separate bowl whisk together your egg, buttermilk, and melted butter until foamy, then add the mix to your flour mix and stir until fully incorporated.

2.Allow your batter to rest for 10 minutes, then heat up a frying pan on medium heat. Add a thin layer of vegetable oil to the pan, then add a 3/4 ladle of the mix directly to the centre of the pan and allow the pancake to form. Once you start to see bubbles appear, flip the pancake and cook until golden brown. Repeat the process until your stack is complete.

Load them with as many or as few of your favourite toppings whether sweet or savoury and enjoy!!

Ingredients:

200g Self Raising Flour
1 tbsp Sugar
¼ tsp Baking Soda
2 tbsp Butter
Vegetable Oil for Pan
Frying

1 Cup of Buttermilk (or ¾ of a cup of milk and a quarter of lemon juice mixed directly into the milk and leave for 10 minutes that will make buttermilk)

VENISON AND SCOTCH BONNET SCOTCH EGGS

2-4 servings

30 minutes

Ingredients:

Sausagemeat Mix:
8 Vension Sausages (or any Good Quality Pork Sausages)
1 Scotch Bonnet Pepper Finely Diced
1 tsp Coarse Grain Mustard
¼ Finely Diced Granny Smith Apple
¼ Finely Diced Red Onion
1 tsp Smoke Paprika
1 tsp Garlic Powder
2 tsp Fresh Chopped Rosemary
2 tbsp Freshly Chopped Parsley
Pinch of Salt and Pepper

Coating:
500g Seasoned Panko and Breadcrumbs
250g Seasoned Flour
2 Eggs Beaten
(Seasoning can either be a pinch of each of the powder spices for the sausagemeat mix or open to your own interpretation)
2 Large Free Range Eggs for Boiling
Greseproof Paper

Steps for Cooking:

Take your sausages out of the packet and carefully slice [do]wn the skin of each sausage, releasing the meat from the [ca]sings. Discard the casings and add all of the [sa]usagemeat into a bowl along with the other sausage [me]at ingredients, cover, and put in the fridge.

[N]ext, bring a large saucepan of water to a boil on medium [hea]t and get a separate bowl full of ice-cold water with ice [cu]bes. As soon as the water comes to a boil, add your two [lar]ge eggs and cook for exactly 6 minutes. Once you have [rea]ched 6 minutes, take the eggs out immediately and get [the]m into the iced water (the iced water will stop the cooking [pr]ocess immediately so your eggs don't overcook).

[N]ext, get your dredging station ready. So, in three separate [bo]wls, you will have: 1. Your seasoned flour; 2. Your beaten [eg]gs; and 3. Your seasoned breadcrumbs (the breadcrumb [bo]wl needs to be nice and deep so you can make a well to [si]t the egg in to make it easier to coat).Next, using a sheet [of] greaseproof paper on a clean work surface, get your [pa]per laid down flat in a square, take your sausage mix out [of] the fridge, and using half of the mix, flatten it out on the [gr]easeproof paper until it is thin enough to cover your egg [bu]t not so thin that it will tear.

[T]hen, run your cold tap and carefully crack the side of one [of] your eggs using the running water, allowing it to get under [th]e shell. Carefully peel away the shell, allowing the water to [he]lp you. Be patient and keep a steady hand until eventually [all] of the shell is removed. Repeat this for both eggs.

5. Next, place your egg carefully in the middle of the flattened sausage meat, and using wet hands, carefully fold and encase the meat around the egg, being as even as possible and cutting away any excess meat as you go, until your egg is protected by the sausage meat.Repeat this process with the second egg.

6.Next, get your oil on medium heat and carefully roll your egg in the flour (this will help the beaten egg to stick), then roll it in the beaten egg (this will help the breadcrumbs to stick) then finally create a well in the middle of your breadcrumbs. Lower the egg in and coat with the crumbs, carefully shaking off any excess so you have an even coating, and set on a board. Repeat the process with the second egg.

7.Now, cooking one at a time, carefully lower your egg into the oil, and again, we want to roll the egg in the oil to keep the outer crumb a nice, even colour, and again, we want to cook the egg for 6 minutes total to keep the egg in the middle nice and gooey.

8.Once cooked, drain on a wire rack or paper towel, and repeat the process with your second egg. Once they have both been cooked and cooled slightly, slice them in half carefully to reveal that perfect yolk, and serve with a selection of your favourite chutneys and pickles.

Notes

I used to have a mate who loved lunchtime at school, but he only ever ate the same thing ..... Good old Scott Chegg Enjoy guys!!

HOT AS CLUCK WINGS

 2-4 servings   30 minutes

Ingredients:

½ Kilo of Chicken Drummettes

For the Butter milk:
750ml of Whole Milk
250ml of Lemon Juice
Salt and Pepper
2 tbsp Hot Sauce

For the Seasoning:
1 tbsp Garlic Salt
1 tbsp Mixed Pepperorns Ground
1 tbsp Dried Oregano
1 tbsp Onion Powder
1 tbsp Smoked Paprika
1 tbsp Grated Lemon Zest
1 Chicken Stock Cube Crumbled
2 tsp Cayenne Pepper

For the Batter:
2 Eggs
500g of Plain Flour
1 tbsp Crushed Red Chilli Flakes
1 tsp Cayenne Pepper
1 tbsp Hot Sauce
Salt and Pepper
Good Quality Oil for Deep Frying

Garnish Options:
Chopped Spring Onion/Pink
Pickled Onions/Coriander, Freshly
Chopped Chillies, Sesame Seeds,
Hot Sauce, and American Mustard
(or go with your personal
preference).

Steps for Cooking:

1.Pour your buttermilk into a deep dish and add your hot sauce, salt, and pepper (if using pre-made buttermilk, pour it straight in; if not, pour your milk into a large bowl/jug add your lemon juice mix together, and leave for 10 minutes; don't worry about the weird-looking consistency; it's meant to be like that) and give it a good mix. Add your wings to the buttermilk so they're completely covered, cover your dish, and pop it in the fridge to marinade (minimum 2 hours, ideally overnight).

2.Next, mix together all of your seasoning ingredients in a large bowl. Take the wings out of the fridge and take them out of the buttermilk one at a time. Coat them in your seasoning. Shake off any excess seasoning as you go and arrange them neatly on a board.

3.Next, get your flour into a shallow bowl, season with a pinch of salt and pepper, and mix. In a separate bowl, whisk together your eggs, hot sauce, chilli flakes, and cayenne pepper.

4.Now, get your oil on medium heat and carefully coat your wings in the egg mixture, then into the flour. Shake off the excess, but ensure that they are coated evenly, and place them in the oil one at a time, turning carefully to ensure even cooking (you should be able to comfortably cook three wings at a time). Drain the wings on a wire rack or a tray with a paper towel. Repeat the process until all the wings are cooked. (When we deep fry, generally speaking, when it floats to the top of the oil, its done, but with poultry, always make sure you're at a temperature of 72 degrees celsius minimum if using a meat thermometer or carefully lift the meat out of the oil and poke it in its thickest part with a knife. If the juices run clear with no blood, then you're good to go).

5.Get your wings on a plate, be as creative as you like with your garnishes and give them bad boys a bite. (Make sure you've got a glass of milk on standby just in case).

Notes

As it goes I tried talking to a chicken once, and it actually spoke back ..... I think I might be bi"wing"ual. Enjoy guys!!

TOAD IN THE HOLE WITH CARAMELISED RED ONION GRAVY

2-4 servings 1 hour

Ingredients:

Thick Cut Good Quality
Sausages
Large Red Onion cut in
Half then each half into 4
Sprigs of Fresh Thyme
Sprigs of Fresh
Rosemary
Tbsp Olive Oil
Salt and Pepper to Taste

For the Yorkshire:
5g Plain Flour
ml Milk
Eggs
tsp Nutmeg
Salt and Pepper to taste

For the Gravy:
3 Large Red Onions
Finely Sliced
2 Cloves of Garlic
Finely Sliced
1 tbsp Demerara
Sugar
2 Sprigs of Thyme
1 tbsp Olive Oil
1 tbsp Dark Soy
500ml Good Quality
Beef/Chicken Stock

Steps for Cooking:

1.In a large bowl, add your flour, nutmeg, salt, and pepper, and whisk together. Create a well in the middle of the flour mix and crack in three eggs. Gently whisk together until fully incorporated, then carefully add your milk in bit by bit while whisking continuously until you have a smooth, silky batter (you can add a bit more flour and whisk it in if you accidentally overdid the milk; just remember to adjust your seasoning). Transfer the batter into a jug and cover before popping it in the fridge (the batter can be made the night before, ideally but 30minutes in advance is fine)

2.Next, preheat your oven to gas mark 6, and in a large, deep skillet or frying pan (it needs to be big enough so that there is plenty of room between your ingredients for the Yorkshire batter to get between), add 3 tbsp of olive oil and get it on medium heat, then add your sausages, rosemary, and thyme, and red onion wedges, ensuring that you turn the sausages regularly to achieve an even brown, and turn the onions until they are caramelised, then add another 3 tbsp of olive oil to the pan.

3.Next, take your Yorkshire pudding batter out of the fridge and give it a good mix. Take the rosemary and thyme stalks out of the pan before pouring the batter in one spot between the ingredients. Do not be tempted to move the jug; keep pouring, and the batter will eventually fill the gaps between the ingredients. You can tilt the pan once you have poured the batter in to ensure it's even if you wish.

4.Next, get the pan straight into the oven on the middle shelf and cook for 35 minutes, or until the batter is risen and golden brown.

5.While the toad in the hole is cooking, let's start the gravy. So, in a deep based saucepan get your oil on medium heat and get all of your red onions into the pan. Coat them in the oil, then allow them to soften for 5 minutes before adding your garlic, thyme, and sugar. Coat the onions again before letting them caramelise for another 15 minutes. Add your dark soy, then your stock, and let the gravy reduce on a low/medium simmer until you get your preferred consistency.

Notes

Get your toad in the hole out of the oven, get that gorgeous gravy in a serving jug, and you can serve this up with some of your favourite vegetables. In the picture, I have used my honey-roasted carrot recipe, which is also in this book, and a bit of cabbage sauteed in olive oil and butter and finished in the oven, but again, it's your dish; you have any vegetables you like.

Now, I know you're all waiting for a joke, but .. Toad in the Hole .... I'm gonna leave that one to your imagination. Enjoy guys!!

POSH GAMMON EGG, CHIPS AND PEAS

 2-4 servings   🕐 30 minutes

Ingredients:

2 Good Quality Gammon
Steaks
2 Pineapple Rings
2 tbsp Olive Oil
Cracked Black Pepper
1 Large Free Range Egg
Good Quality Oil for Shallow
Frying

For the Chips:
3 Maris Piper Potatoes
Good quality Oil for Deep Frying

For the Pea Puree:
500g Frozen Peas
Juice of 1 Lemon
A good pinch of salt and pepper
Small handful of freshly chopped
parsley

For the Jus (Gravy):
1 Banana Shallot Finely Diced
1 tbsp Plain Flour
2 tbsp Butter
1 tsp White Wine Vinegar
250ml Good quality Chicken Stock
1 tsp Worcestershire Sauce
1 tsp Coarse Grain Mustard
1 tbsp Fresh Thyme Leaves

Steps for Cooking:

1.Peel and chop your potatoes into chips,then soak them in a bowl of cold water for 30 minutes to release any excess starch. Once soaked, get them into a saucepan of salted water to blanch. Once blanched, get your chips drained, then onto a tray and into the freezer for one hour.

2.Get a pan of salted water on medium heat and blanch your peas for 3 minutes before removing them from the water with a slotted spoon into a bowl. Then add your peas and fresh parsley to a blender along with a good pinch of salt and pepper, and using the water you blanched the peas in, add a little bit at a time while pulsing your peas until you have a thick puree. Spoon the puree into a fine sieve and push it through using the back of a ladle to give you a nice smooth finish, then add your lemon juice a bit at a time, mixing well until you're happy with the result, and set aside.

3.Now, pre-heat your oven to Gas Mark 4, and get your deep-frying oil on medium heat for your chips. Take your chips out of the freezer and fry on medium heat until they start to brown. Get them on some paper towels to drain, and take your oil off the heat for now.

4.Next, get a skillet/frying pan on a medium/high heat, and as soon as it starts to smoke, add a touch of oil. Get your gammon steaks in the pan, seasoning well with black pepper as they cook (they are salty already, so just using black pepper is fine). Cook your gammon for 3 minutes either side, then get your pan in the oven and get some oil in a small frying pan for your fried egg on low heat (the oil should reach just below the yolk).

5.Next, get your deep frying oil back on the gas on high heat, crack your egg on a flat surface carefully so you don break the yolk directly into the centre of the oil in your small frying pan, and allow the egg to gently fry while you add your chips to the deep frying oil for a second time. Once they're golden brown, get them out of the oil, drain them on some paper towel on a tray, then remove the paper towel and put the tray of chips on the bottom shelf of the oven to keep warm. Your egg will be done at this point, so get it out of the oil using a fish slice straight ont a plate with some paper towel, and season well with salt and pepper.

6.Next, take your gammon out of the oven and cover loosely with some tin foil. Then, using the same pan the gammon was cooked in, get it on medium heat (being careful of the handle as it will be hot from the oven), add splash of oil, then fry your shallot with your thyme leaves before adding your butter, then your flour, and whisk together continuously while adding your chicken stock bi by bit, followed by the rest of the jus ingredients, until you are happy with the consistency, and leave on a low simmer.

7.Now, we are ready to plate. Again, this is open to interpretation. I plated mine by smearing the pea puree onto the plate, then adding the chips, followed by the pineapple ring for stability. Then I sliced the gammon and placed it on top of the pineapple, then finished it with the fried egg, so when you cut into the yolk, it drips down the whole stack. Drizzle with your jus and voila. Level up Gammon egg chips and peas.

Notes

It was hard making this dish because I used to have an addiction to ham .... I'm alright now, though .. I'm fully cured. Enjoy guys!

CHICKEN BALTI PIE WITH A CHEESY BOMBAY POTATO TOP

 2-4 servings   🕐 1 hour

Steps for Cooking:

In a deep saucepan/balti pot, get your dry spices on low heat, shaking gently so they don't catch on the pan until you start to smell their aroma. Turn the heat up to low/medium and add your oil, onions, fresh chillies, lime zest, and coriander stalks. Cook until the onion is caramelised then add your powdered spices and give everything a good mix.

Next, add your ginger-garlic paste and cook for another 5 minutes before adding your chicken and cooking until the chicken is sealed. Then add your peppers and cook for another 5 minutes before adding your tinned tomatoes and passata. Add 125 ml of water to the pot, give it a mix, and cover with a lid to simmer on a low/medium heat.

Next, get your potatoes to a boil in some salted water. Once boiled, drain and mash with the bombay potato ingredients and set aside. Pre-heat your oven to gas mark 5.

Next, get your oil for your carrots on medium heat in a small saucepan and colour the carrots before adding your mango chutney to the pan. As the chutney begins to break down, use it as a glaze to spoon over the carrots before adding a splash of water to the pan, turning the heat to low, and covering with a lid to let the carrots steam for 5 minutes, then take off the heat.

Next, get your chicken off the heat, take out the cinnamon stick, the star anise, and the cardamom pod, squeeze in your lime juice, mix, and allow to cool for 15 minutes before adding the balti into your pie dishes (fill them about half way), then scoop your bombay potato mash on top, sprinkle with your cheese, and poke one of the carrots securely into the top of the pie. Bake for 30 minutes on gas mark 5 or until beautifully browned. Once done, finish with a sprinkling of fresh coriander.

Notes

My serving suggestion for this is ... jump right in these pies don't need any sides.

I made this for my mate the other day, and now he's gone and entered himself into the Indian Olympics.... check him out guys.. his name's Usain Balti. Enjoy!!

Ingredients:

For the Chicken Balti:
4 Large Chicken Breats Diced and Marinated in 1 tsp Salt, 1 tsp chilli Powder, 1 tsp Garam Masala, 1 tsp Turmeric and the Juice of Half a Lemon
3 tbsp Olive Oil

For the Sauce:
Dry Spices
1 tsp Coriander Seeds
1 tsp Mustard Seeds
1 Cinnamon Stick
1 Cardamom Pod
1 Star Anise
2 Cloves

Powder Spices
1 tsp Turmeric
2 tsp Garam Masala
2 tsp Hot Chilli Powder
2 tsp Curry Powder
2 tsp Coriander Powder

2 Medium Red Onions Diced
3 tbsp Ginger Garlic Paste
4 Freshly Chopped Green Birdseye Chillies
2 Tins Chopped Tomatoes
250ml Passata
Chopped Coriander Stalks
1 Red 1 Green Pepper Roughly Diced
Zest and Juice of 1 Lime
Salt to Taste
Fresh Coriander Leaves Finely Chopped

For the Bombay Potato Top:
4 Large Potatoes (King Edward or Maris Piper) Diced
1 tsp Mustard Seeds
1 tsp Garam Masala
1 tsp Curry Powder
2 tsp Turmeric
1 Small Finely Diced Shallot
1 Raw Egg Yolk
Salt to Taste

For the Mango Chutney Roasted Carrots:
4 Chantenay Carrots
1 tbsp Mango Chutney
1 tbsp Olive Oil
Sprinkle of Chilli Flake (Optional)
Grated Mozzarella/Emmental Cheese

CHICKEN TIKKA WITH GARLIC AND CORIANDER NAAN

Steps for Cooking:

Naan

1. Firstly, we need to activate the yeast, which will give the naan that amazing, fluffy texture. We do this by pouring the warm water into a bowl (not too hot as it will kill the yeast, so just above room temperature will be fine), then sprinkling the sugar and yeast into the water and giving it a whisk until fully incorporated, then leave it for 10-15minutes until the mixture turns frothy and has bubbles on top (yeast generally comes in 7g sachets in a box, so you won't need to measure it out).

2. Heat your milk; it will only take 60 seconds, as you don't want to bring it to the boil. Just keep it warm.

3. Add your flour and salt to a mixing bowl and mix together. Make a well in the middle, crack your egg in, and mix again until incorporated.

4. Add in the yeast mixture a bit at a time while stirring to incorporate, along with the milk (again bit by bit), honey, and natural yoghurt, until you form a pliable dough (if the mixture is sticky, don't worry, it's meant to be). Sprinkle your Nigella seeds over the dough and slowly work them through with your hand, being gentle and not overworking the dough (keeping your hands wet will make the whole process a lot easier).

Ingredients:

For the Naan: (Makes 4)
50ml Warm Water
7g Active Dry Yeast
1 tsp Granulated Sugar
200g Plain Flour
½ tsp Salt
1 Egg
1 tsp Honey
6 tbsp Natural Yoghurt
75ml Warm Milk
1 tbsp Extra Virgin Olive il
1 tsp Nigella Seeds
Garlic and Coriander Butter
20g Butter
1 tbsp Minced Garlic
Handful of Freshly Chopped Coriander

For the Chicken:
1 Whole Chicken
1 Litre Tub Natural Yoghurt
1 Lemon
½ Lime
1 Bunch Fresh Coriander
1 Scotch Bonnet
6 Birdseye chillies
2 tsp chilli Flake
2 tsp Turmeric
2 tsp Coriander Powder
1 tbsp Tikka Curry Paste
2 tsp Smoked Parika
1 tbsp Ginger Garlic Paste
2 tbsp Garam Masala
1 tsp chilli Powder
2 Star Anise

For the Green Chutney:
1 Bunch Coriander
2 Green Chillies
½ Lime
Olive Oil
Salt
½ The Tub of Yoghurt from the Chicken

Now, this step is quite tricky, but with wet hands, ke the dough out of the bowl, and rather than eading, you need to pick the dough up and slap it ck down again on a clean work surface. You can use scraper if you need, but you'll need to do this for out 5 minutes until the dough becomes smooth ain. It'll still be sticky but more manageable.

Drizzle the olive oil over the dough and gently assage it in until the dough becomes sticky again, d place into a large greased bowl (pour a tiny bit of into a bowl and wipe it around the base and sides ing a piece of kitchen towel so it's thinly coated and en). It won't be a perfect ball shape at this point, but at's fine. Cover the bowl tightly with cling film and ve somewhere warm to rise. This will take 2-3 urs, depending on the room temperature at the time.

Once risen, empty it into a mixing bowl and add a rinkling of flour if needed (a bit at a time to bring it gether to a dough-like consistency), then grease your nds with a bit of oil and cut the dough into 4 equal eces.

Cover the 4 equal pieces loosely with a clean damp a towel and get your pan on medium-high heat eally something cast iron, as it will help get you to a gher heat than a non-stick pan). Then take one of the ugh balls on a lightly floured surface, push and retch into an oval shape before shaking off any cess flour, gently sprinkling some water onto one de, and putting that side down in the pan first.

Cook on that side and flip after 30–45 seconds, then move the pan from the flame and use the naked me to cook the other side, moving it carefully around achieve a nice even char and the signature naan bbles (only use this technique if you're confident ough; if not, turning the heat up full blast in the pan ce you flip the naan will get you close enough).

Then just repeat the same process with the remaining naans. Of course, if you want to make double the amount of naans, just double the amount of ingredients with the same method.

10.For your garlic and coriander butter, just heat the butter in a small saucepan over low heat so the butter doesn't brown. Add your garlic and continue to cook on low heat until your kitchen smells like an Indian takeaway. Then add your fresh coriander and brush generously over your delicious fluffy charred naan breads (chop a chilli on top aswell if you're feeling adventurous).

Chicken

1.If you can get an already spatchcocked chicken from your butcher, that will save time, but if not, you can get a whole family-sized chicken.

2.To Spatchcock it, simply lay the bird on its front breast side down and locate the backbone (the long bone that starts at the neck down to the rear), and carefully, using a knife with a bit of flexibility, cut down either side of the bone from the top down to the bottom, keeping the knife as close to the bone as possible.

3.Remove the back bone (this can be kept for chicken stock for your next Sunday roast) and apply pressure by pushing down on the back of the bird so it flattens out, then flip over so the breast is facing upwards, and you will have a spatchcocked chicken.

4.Next, you need to score the bird, so using a sharp knife, make slits across the legs, breasts, and wings, ensuring that you don't go too deep, as this will dry the bird out during cooking. You're only looking to slash the skin if possible.

5.Next, in a bowl, add half of the natural yoghurt, ginger-garlic paste, all of your dry powder spices, and

slits and under the skin so it's completely covered, then cover it in a fresh bowl if needed with cling film and pop it in the fridge (minimum 2 hours, but you can do this a day in advance; the longer you leave it, the more tender the meat and flavourful the outcome).

6.Once mixed, using your hands, lather the chicken in the marinade, making sure you get into all the gaps and slits and under the skin so it's completely covered, then cover it in a fresh bowl if needed with cling film and pop it in the fridge (minimum 2 hours, but you can do this a day in advance; the longer you leave it, the more tender the meat and flavourful the outcome).

7.Once the chicken is marinated, get your oven preheated to gas mark 6 (feel free to lay some leftover vegetables on the bottom if you have them, red onions, peppers, etc., drizzled with a bit of olive oil), then place your chicken on top, the lemon that you grated the zest from, pop that in as well whole (it will help to tenderise the meat further during the cooking process), your Scotch Bonnet pepper (whole), and your Star anise, and pop it in the oven for an hour and a half, basting with the juices as you go.

Take the chicken out (check to see if it's cooked by piercing the meat between the leg and breast at its thickest part; if the juices run clear with no red, it's done) or if you have a meat thermometer, it needs to be a minimum of 72 degrees.

8.Cover the cooked chicken with loose foil and allow it to rest. Resting will keep the juices in the meat, so when you carve it, it will be tender and moist. While rests you can do your chutney.

Green Chutney

In a food processor, blender, or even smoothie mak blitz up your coriander stalks and all with your green chilli and lime (including zest) and add your oil bit b bit until you have a vibrant green sauce. Add your sa give it one more blitz, then pour into the other half o the yoghurt you used for your chicken, give it a good mix, pour it into a lovely serving dish, get the rest of the coriander chopped, and over your chicken, lathe up your naans with that gorgeous garlic butter and enjoy!

PEANUT BUTTER POPCORN

VEGETARIAN OPTION FRIENDLY

 2-4 servings

 15 minutes

Ingredients:

60g Popping Corn Kernels	1 tsp Vanilla Essence
1 tbsp Vegetable Oil	2 tbsp Crunchy Peanut Butter
2 tbsp Honey	Sea Salt Flakes

Steps for cooking:

1.Get your oil into a deep-based saucepan with a lid. While uncovered on low-medium heat, add three popcorn kernels to the oil and wait until all three have popped (this means the oil is hot enough and the rest of the popcorn will cook evenly then get the rest of the popcorn in and cover with a lid whilst shaking the pan above the flame carefully until the popping sound stops, then pour your popcorn onto a tray.

2.Next, in the same saucepan on low heat, add your honey and peanut butter to the pan with a pinch of sea salt and mix continuously until fully melted.

3.Take off the heat, add your vanilla essence, give it a final stir, and pour the sauce over your popcorn. Mix well with a wooden spoon, coating the popcorn as evenly as possible.

4.Get your popcorn into bowls, finish them with another sprinkling of salt, and enjoy.

Printed in Great Britain
by Amazon